PORTRAIT OF T

Fifty years of bi1
Christchurch Park, Ipswich

**Reg Snook
with Philip Murphy**

Illustrations by Reg Snook

Edited by
Ann Snook and Richard Wilson

Gresham

First Published in 2014 by Gresham Publications
in association with
The Friends of Christchurch Park, Ipswich

www.focp.org.uk

Text © 2014 Reg Snook
Illustrations © 2014 Reg Snook

All rights reserved. No part of this book may be reprinted or reproduced or utilised in any form or by any electronic, mechanical or other means, now known or hereafter invented, including photocopying and recording, or in any information storage or retrieval system, without permission in writing from the author.

A catalogue record of this book is available from the British Library

Snook, Reg
Portrait of the Birds

Printed by Tuddenham Press Ltd.

ISBN 978-0-9561080-3-6

The other books by Reg Snook in the *Portrait* trilogy are

Portrait of a Park
A year with the wildlife of Christchurch Park

Portrait of an Owl
My tales of Mabel and other owls

For more details on these and other books published by
the Friends of Christchurch Park go to
www.focp.org.uk

ACKNOWLEDGEMENTS

I should like to acknowledge Philip Murphy's extensive contribution to this book, which couldn't have been written without his knowledge and insight. My thanks as ever to Ann Snook for her help and support in producing this third book in the *Portrait* trilogy, and also to Richard Wilson for his time and expertise in preparing the text for publication.

A short-eared owl being mobbed by crows

Contents

About the authors 1
Introduction 4
Common birds of the Park 9
Birds we have lost 13
Birds we have gained 17
Waterbirds and waders 19
Mandarin duck 22
Sparrowhawk and kestrel 25
Pigeons of the Park 30
Mabel, our tawny owl 35
Woodpeckers 39
Spotted flycatcher 43
Treecreeper and nuthatch 45
The crow family 48
Winter and summer visitors 51
Scarce visitors 54
Birds flying over the Park 58
What of the future? 61
List of birds observed in or seen flying over the Park 68
Index 71

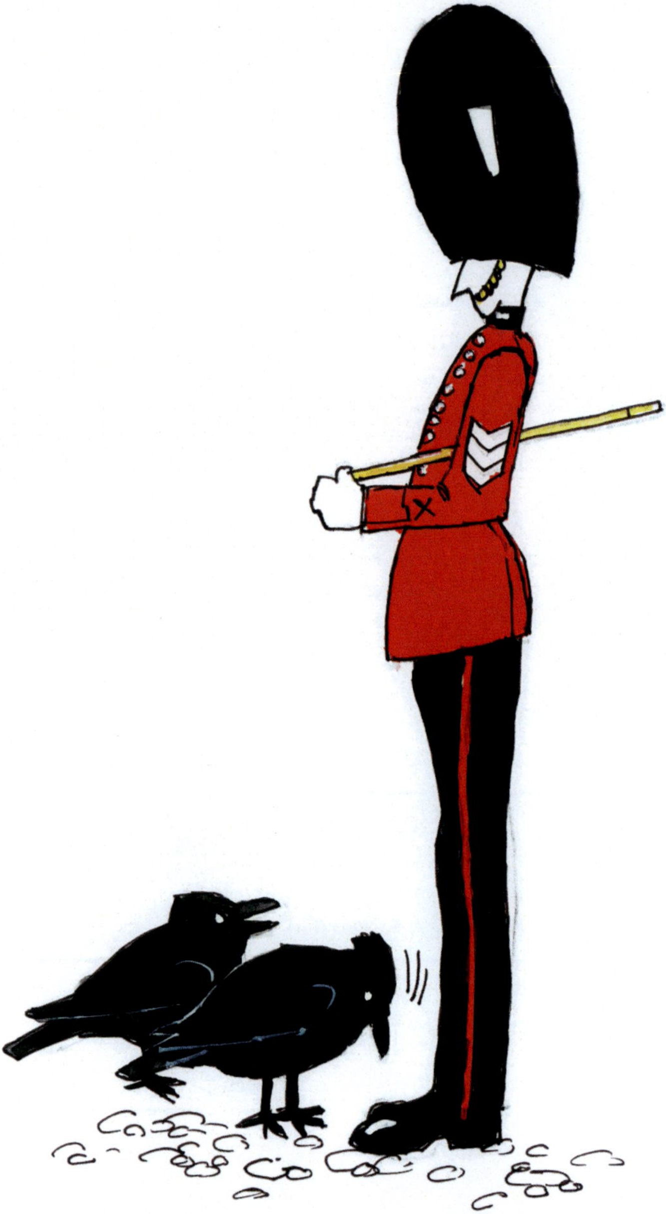

ABOUT THE AUTHORS

Reg Snook's interest in wildlife was fostered in the years following the Second World War when the countryside was a wonderful place in which a young boy could roam. This led to a lifelong interest in wildlife, especially birds.

National Service then got in the way. The Grenadier Guards wanted him although he didn't particularly want the Grenadiers. At least it got him to Africa where, when not fighting terrorists, he was able to study the beautiful birds of west Africa. A return to England meant swapping touracos and palm-nut vultures for cockney sparrows and ravens at the Tower of London. Public duties were now on the agenda; Trooping the Colour and guard mounting at Buck and Jimmies Palaces, full of pomp and smartness. The Grenadiers were the first Guards to move from Wellington Barracks to the newly-built Chelsea Barracks (now no longer an Army establishment). On guard mounting mornings he would swagger down Ebury Road to Buck House, often to the tune of *They're changing guard at Buckingham Palace*. A. A. Milne's words often made him smile: "We saw a guard in a sentry-box. 'One of the sergeants looks after their socks,' says Alice." Yeah, right Alice! But guard mounting at the Tower of London was great; Reg could study and sketch the ravens.

Alongside Philip Murphy, Reg was a founder member in 1973 of the Suffolk Ornithologists' Group, and for 30 years from 1982 to 2012 a DEFRA Wildlife Inspector specialising in birds of prey. The Inspectorate was instrumental in reducing the numbers of birds of prey illegally taken from the wild both in this country and abroad.

Philip Murphy's links with Christchurch Park began in late 1974 when daily journeys to work in central Ipswich took him through the Park. This continued for 11 years resulting in Philip obtaining a wealth of ornithological information. Observations resumed in the late 1990s but on a slightly less regular basis depending on when his daughter, Naomi, wanted to play in the Park...

Both Philip and Reg attended Northgate Grammar School for Boys in Ipswich, but Reg left the year Philip was born! Reg and Philip first became acquainted in 1973 when they became founder members of the Suffolk Ornithologists' Group. Philip's headmaster at Northgate, the late Denis Ockelton, was later to become the SOG's Chairman.

For the last 33 years Philip has been part of the editorial team that produces the annual *Suffolk Bird Report*, ensuring that it features notable observations from Christchurch Park. His dedication to recording local birdlife and his unstinting work for the SOG has been rewarded with him becoming one of its Honorary Vice-Presidents.

Since that original meeting in 1973 Philip and Reg have become firm birding friends, and for over 40 years they have been recording and swapping bird notes, mainly about the birds of Christchurch Park.

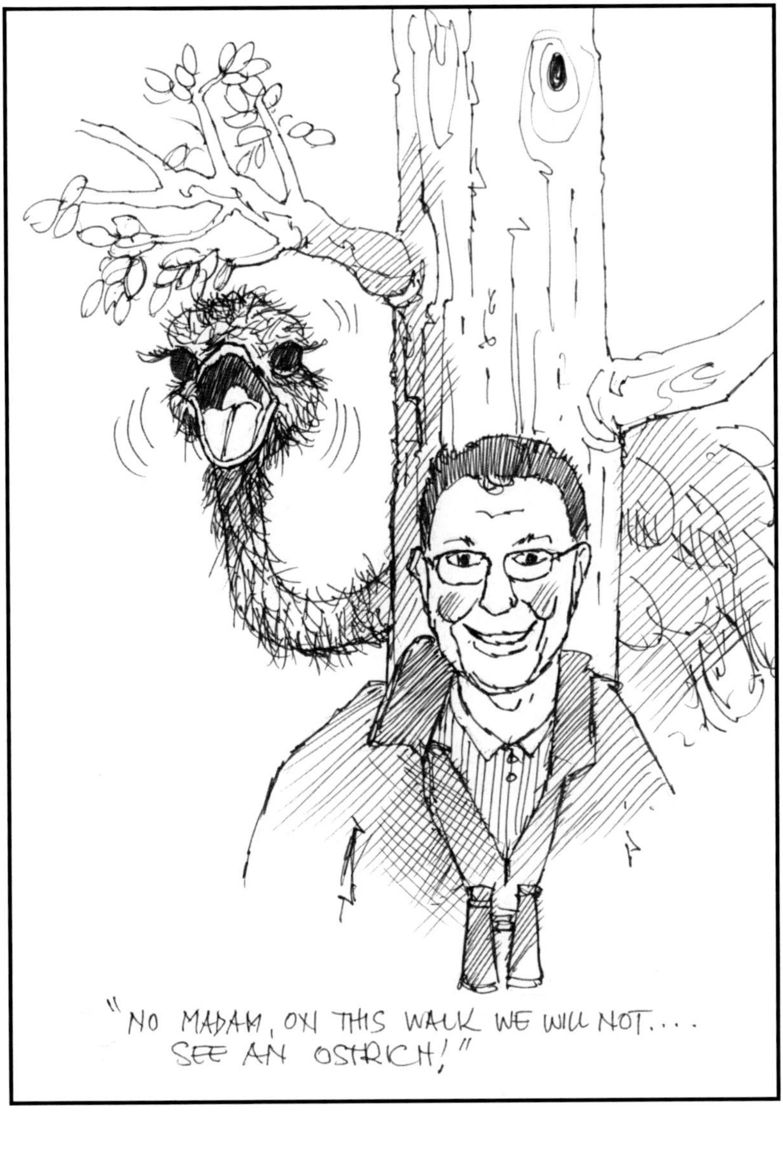
"NO MADAM, ON THIS WALK WE WILL NOT....
SEE AN OSTRICH!"

INTRODUCTION

It can be said that there are two main species of birdwatcher – those who chase after rarities and those who concentrate their attention on one particular site. Ipswich has a population of approximately 135,000 and, with Christchurch Park being in the centre of the town, some might suggest that the Park is not a site worth studying. How wrong can that be?

This final book in the *Portrait* trilogy acknowledges the recordings of the Park's birds carried out over the past 50 years. During the time we have been monitoring the birds here there have been enormous changes in both species and numbers of birds. This book documents these important changes – it would have been a lost opportunity if the history of Christchurch Park's birdlife had not been so documented.

Some species have disappeared and others have recently arrived, as has happened elsewhere in Suffolk. The birds, indeed all the wildlife of Christchurch Park, have had to adapt to sharing their lives with thousands of people who in turn think of this area as being their own recreational ground.

Christchurch Park extends over 33 hectares (approximately 82 acres) of beautiful undulating land just north of the former old town wall. The Park dates back to the 12th century when the Augustinian Priory of the Holy Trinity (also known as Christ Church) was founded. The magnificent Grade I listed Mansion was built in 1548-50 on the site of the dissolved Priory.

The Park has varied habitats including open grassland, formal borders in the Upper and Lower Arboretums, bowling greens, ponds and dense woodland. It is dotted with several old and veteran trees including 300 to 400 year-old oaks and sweet chestnuts. But the Park also hosts more and more events, meaning that the pressures on wildlife are enormous. Every weekend during the summer Ip-Art festival (with attractions such as Global Rhythm, the Big Top and the open-air cinema) our bird life must endure many disturbances. The ever-popular Music Day sees the Park divided into sections for all types of bands and their music, and attracts (it is estimated) over 40,000 people on this one day alone. The music is usually very loud – though not nearly as loud as the annual firework extravaganza in November! Does this mean that wildlife no longer has a place in Christchurch Park? Not a bit of it.

After the great storm of 1987, a section of woodland adjacent to the Wilderness Pond was fenced off and designated as a Bird Reserve. Notices informing the public of what could be seen there were placed at the entrances and, although there has been a certain amount of vandalism and abuse over time, it is still there 25 years later. Now named the Wildlife Reserve it is what it says it is – a haven for wildlife. There is also the Wilderness Pond, a natural water feature (the Park's many springs have served the town and wildlife well over the centuries), where eight species of duck have been recorded. In 2007 the pond was emptied and cleared of silt and sludge as part of the Heritage Lottery Restoration Project, and it is now deep enough for roach to breed in it successfully.

Since 2005, cormorants have taken up residence, drastically reducing fish numbers especially in the nearby Round Pond where the magnificent goldfish have now all but disappeared. The cormorant is one of the Park's newest arrivals as is the lesser black-backed gull, a bird of great beauty but also one that has recently prevented the duck population, including another relative newcomer the mandarin duck, from having much breeding success. Now recognised as a British wild bird, the mandarin is a colourful addition to the Park and is perhaps the gaudiest of all British wildfowl. Its history in Christchurch Park is documented in the Friends of Christchurch Park's previous book *Portrait of a Park*.

The Park lost its rookery in the tall chestnut trees at the back of Bethesda Church after 1978. With Ipswich's ever-expanding boundaries the rooks probably had difficulty in finding sufficient food for their young. Five species of crow have been recorded in Christchurch Park. It is interesting that local personality Percy Edwards, the famous bird mimic, heard his first ravens here. They became his inspiration, though it is unfortunate that the ravens were captive birds in a menagerie near Christchurch Mansion. With changes in attitudes this menagerie and its ravens are just a memory, and, sadly, Percy too is no longer with us. Strangely, ravens are now gradually spreading throughout East Anglia and perhaps in the not-too-distant future we might hear wild ravens calling again, not from cages, but from the Scots pines in the Wildlife Reserve.

With its varied landscape of grassy slopes, wooded areas and assorted ponds, Christchurch Park offers a number of different habitats for wildlife. An added bonus is that the adjacent houses have large established gardens where many of the Park's resident birds choose to breed. Although the Park is visited by thousands of people it is still a birdwatching paradise.

Nesting blackbirds

COMMON BIRDS OF THE PARK

There is much in this book about rarer birds and those that have become the Park's specialities (such as the tawny owl and mandarin for example), but we mustn't overlook our more common birds – the ones we might take for granted. Often it is these common species that are an indication of whether "all is right with the world" or whether something is going drastically wrong. If a species is in decline then there has to be a reason, even if it may not be obvious. With many species that are declining, the phrase "climate change" is all-too-often used but, how many of us know what the term really means? It is suggested that an increase in temperature of one or two degrees could easily affect some species due to a loss of insect food when nesting takes place. Insectivorous birds need insects for their young. The disastrous disappearance of red-back shrikes from Suffolk (and indeed from Britain) has been put down to climate change, so too the decline of the spotted flycatcher.

It is easy to understand a bird's disappearance through change or lack of habitat, but when the habitat in which a bird has flourished seemingly remains the same, finding a reason for its decline can be difficult. We are certain that many of our Park's more common birds suffer greatly from both predation and disturbance. They have many predators ranging from sparrowhawks to corvids, from grey squirrels to cats and of course the Park is used for many more public activities now, especially in the summer. We have tried to give a reason as to why the Park's nuthatches are down to a single pair (maybe not even that) whilst at the same time a somewhat similar bird, the treecreeper, appears to be on the increase. Likewise, most probably because of predation by large gulls, we are fully aware that our waterfowl numbers have plummeted in recent years. However, it is more difficult to judge whether or not our most common birds are in fact maintaining their numbers.

One of the best ways of counting songbirds is to listen in the spring and summer to singing males. By this measure we know that the most common Park birds, mistle thrush, blackbird, robin, dunnock, blue tit, great tit and wren, are in a healthy position. The majority of the bird boxes positioned by the Friends of Christchurch Park in the Wildlife Reserve have been occupied by blue tits and great tits. They are also used by wrens, now considered to be the most common songbird in Britain.

The relatively strong numbers of these various songbirds may also be due to Christchurch Park being surrounded on three of its sides by large gardens where they like to nest and where food is readily available. If this is the case then activities in the Park will not affect these common birds too much even though the past 50 years have seen a huge increase in human visitors to the Park. More and more people have their own transport and therefore it is not just locals who exercise their dogs, bring a picnic or walk through on their way to work. The Park is busy every day when the weather is fine, and must absorb thousands of visitors for its events. This in turn means more wear and tear, more litter and much more noise. There was a time when the Bird (now Wildlife) Reserve had a boundary fence, gates and prohibitive signs telling the public to keep their dogs on leads. Now there are no fences or gates, and minuscule warning signs, with too few people treating this area as a special part of the Park. With massive amounts of disturbance and abuse perhaps it is little wonder if the majority of our bird population find the nearby gardens to be a safer sanctuary (even if it means having to be aware of both domestic and feral cats).

It is interesting to note the change in fortune and in the breeding habits of our resident thrushes. The larger of our resident thrushes, the mistle thrush, breeds in the Park. It builds an untidy nest in the fork of a tree and eggs are usually laid before the leaves appear, sometimes as early as February. In late summer, family parties of mistle thrushes are often seen searching for food on the grassy areas near to the ice-cream kiosk or on the wide open spaces at the northern end of the Park.

*The mistle thrush builds its nest
in the fork of a tree*

Families of green woodpeckers can also be seen searching for food in these areas and, because both woodpeckers and mistle thrushes have an upright stance whilst on the ground, the casual observer might find it difficult to tell these two species apart.

Given the number of predators in our Park you might imagine that mistle thrushes would have difficulty in raising any young here at all. An open nest in the fork of a tree with hardly any cover at all surely means easy pickings for magpies and crows? However the mistle thrush is a fierce protector of its eggs and young. When danger appears it is quite fearless, and the loud grating noise of its alarm call is usually sufficient to scare its enemies away.

Fifty years ago blackbirds and song thrushes were common nesters in the Park, many favouring the large area of rhododendrons near the tennis courts in which to build their nests. Song thrushes declined alarmingly in the 1970s and are only now beginning to increase in number again. However, it can still be difficult to find a song thrush's nest in Christchurch Park. Predation by crows, magpies, jays and grey squirrels has seen blackbirds and song thrushes seeking safety in the nearby gardens for their nests. Because of the threat from and lack of control of predator species, Christchurch Park is now a feeding rather than a breeding area for our blackbirds and thrushes.

BIRDS WE HAVE LOST

Bird populations are in a constant state of flux but over the past 50 years we have lost several species from the Park. Lesser spotted woodpeckers have declined dramatically throughout England since the 1980s. Two pairs of this tiny woodpecker were present here in the 1970s and 1980s but none has been reported since 1996. It has been suggested that this national decline might be due to competition with the great spotted woodpecker, predation or declining woodland quality linked to food availability.

For unknown reasons, hawfinches have also declined across Britain since the late 1980s. In the Park, up to four of these large but very elusive finches were noted at infrequent intervals in the Arboretum, but the final sighting was of an agitated pair in 1981.

Tree sparrows were also a feature of the Park in the 1970s. There were a maximum of 15 in 1977 and it seems likely that two pairs bred in the Park up until then. Tree sparrow numbers have plummeted across south eastern England at the same time, possibly because of reduced over-winter survival linked with agricultural changes. None has been noted in the Park since 1979. House sparrows are also now rarely seen in the Park.

Another familiar resident to have disappeared is the bullfinch whose population in Britain has also declined rapidly perhaps due to poor over-winter survival. Groups of up to 12 were recorded in the Park in the 1970s. Single pairs of linnet and lesser redpoll bred in the Park in the mid-1970s but they have not done so since. Both species still occur here occasionally, the linnet mainly as a passage visitor in spring and the lesser redpoll as a scarce winter

*Birds we have lost:
bullfinches on ash keys*

visitor, usually to be seen with siskins in the Park's alder trees.

A close relative of the chaffinch, the brambling is predominantly a winter visitor to Britain from Scandinavia. Groups of up to 30 occurred here regularly in the winter months until the late 1970s but none has been noted since the 1980s. However, it seems likely that a few passage bramblings still pass over the Park in the autumn.

Two species of summer visitor, turtle dove and wood warbler, have also stopped appearing in the Park. The rapid decline of the turtle dove in Britain has been well documented, with possible reasons including agricultural intensification, hunting pressure on migration routes and conditions in the African wintering grounds. A pair possibly bred in the Park in 1977 and in that period it was not unusual to see groups of up to six flying over the Park in the summer months – alas no longer.

Wood warblers used to occur occasionally in the Park in spring but more typically in the autumn. These birds would have either been going to or coming from their breeding grounds to the west or north of East Anglia. None has been noted in the Park for at least 20 years: the reasons for their decline in Britain have again been linked to changes in climate and land use in the African wintering areas.

Undoubtedly the most iconic bird that the Park has lost is the rook. Park goers of more mature years might well remember the rookery in the chestnut trees behind Bethesda Church. This held 10 nests in 1975 but apparently no breeding pairs in 1976, 7 nests in 1977 and then 16 nests in 1978. Nesting has not been noted in the Park since. Problems with food availability and competition with carrion crows could be amongst the reasons for their departure. This demise has been mirrored throughout Ipswich where there have been probably no rookeries for about 15 to 20 years. In the mid-1970s the chestnut trees which contained the rookery also hosted in late-summer evenings a mixed roost of rooks and jackdaws. The number of birds using this roost peaked at about 3,000 in late August and early September 1974. Rooks are now only scarce visitors to the Park but one or two pairs of jackdaws nest annually in sweet chestnut trees close to the Reg Driver Visitor Centre.

MAGPIE

BIRDS WE HAVE GAINED

The most spectacular addition to the list of Park birds in recent years has undoubtedly been the mandarin duck. An account of this duck's status on the Park ponds is presented in a later chapter but it appears that the Park's first record occurred in September 1977. A pair was present in May 1999 and the Park's first brood of ducklings was recorded in May 2000.

It is perhaps surprising to learn that a magpie seen in the Park on 16 January 1975 is the first known site record. Further sightings were made in 1978 and 1982 after which the species became a regular occurrence. A roost of magpies developed in the evergreen oaks behind the former croquet lawn, which peaked at 35 birds in December 2006.

Magpies are renowned predators of birds' eggs and nestlings. Another predator that the Park has gained is the sparrowhawk. Agricultural chemicals decimated this raptor in the 1950s and 60s but the sparrowhawk has been steadily increasing since that time. The first Park record for the period under review was of a female on 11 September 1978 but the species did not become established in the Park until the late 1990s.

Much has been written in recent years of the damaging effect of herring gulls and lesser black-backed gulls on young ducks, geese and moorhens on ponds such as our own. In the 1970s and 80s these two gull species were noted only as they flew over the Park on their way to and from feeding sites elsewhere. However, in the 1990s they commenced nesting on the roofs of large industrial and retail sites in Ipswich. Eventually they moved to domestic properties to nest, taking advantage of plentiful supplies of discarded food. The nesting gulls inevitably found their way into the Park, much to the detriment of our waterfowl. The lesser black-backed gulls (below) are mainly present in the summer months because many spend the winter in Iberia or north-western Africa and come here to breed. Herring gulls are seen in the Park throughout the year.

It can be inferred from all this that most of the birds we have gained might be classed as aggressive predators.

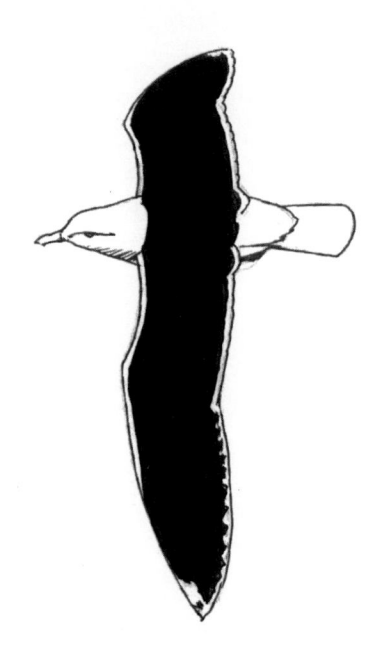

WATERBIRDS AND WADERS

The water birds which inhabit the Park's ponds have attracted much attention over the years, especially the three principal residents: the Canada goose, mallard and moorhen.

In the spring of 2014 it was thought that five pairs of Canada geese were present in the Park, but the population was much higher in the early years of the 21st century – 75 being present in October 2005. That year there was also a count of about 100 mallard on the ponds. In November 2005, a female mallard accompanied by three tiny ducklings was present on the Wilderness Pond as late as 9 November.

Counts of moorhens peaked at 30 on 5 November 2004 and in 1976 an adult moorhen accompanied by three tiny juveniles was noted on the Wilderness Pond as late as 2 November. One or two greylag geese occasionally accompany the Canada geese. In 1976, a female greylag goose paired with a male Canada goose and produced three goslings.

A pair of mute swans frequented the Round Pond in the 1960s but the species has since been irregular in its visits. An adult was present between February and June 2005 on the Round Pond. A juvenile and two adults also delighted observers in December 2010 and January 2011 with the adults lingering on until February.

A magnificent adult lesser white-fronted goose, presumably an escapee from a wildfowl collection, was an unexpected visitor to the Round Pond on 28 September 2005.

A pair of Muscovy ducks was present on the ponds in the late 1970s, and in March 1977 a female was accompanied by four ducklings. There have been at least three sightings of single tufted ducks on the ponds over the years and occasional sightings of shelduck and shoveler.

Other wildfowl to have been recorded on the ponds are a little grebe on the Wilderness Pond in February 2004, a female or immature teal in September 1977, a male Carolina in May 2008 and a female or immature goosander in January 2014. Photographs of the latter bird featured in the local media and on birdwatching websites probably making it second only to Mabel, our resident tawny owl, in the list of most photographed birds in the Park.

The commonest gull on the ponds is the black-headed gull. This gull is present in appreciable numbers between July and March when the adults depart for their breeding grounds in eastern Europe and southern Scandinavia. A few immatures and non-breeders remain throughout the spring and summer. Adults and juveniles start to return in July but it is not until the mid-winter months that the year's highest totals are recorded: for example 175 on 20 November 2005. During the winter, maximum daily totals are present in late afternoons as birds that have been feeding further inland stop off to bathe and preen on the Park's ponds before moving on to roost on the Orwell estuary.

Herons are very infrequent visitors to the Wilderness Pond but are regularly seen flying overhead. Kingfishers were also noted quite regularly at the Wilderness Pond before the Heritage Lottery clearance and de-silting work but much less so since then. There were reports several years ago of a pair of kingfishers breeding there but this was never proven.

It is remarkable that no less than seven species of wader have been noted flying over the Park. Lapwings were still a common species in the 1970s when a record total of 220 flew west over the Park on 30 January 1976. In the same decade there were five sightings of single common snipe. A whimbrel flew north-east on 7 May 1976 and a common sandpiper was seen in the Upper Arboretum in July 1973. Three golden plover flew north on 6 August 1977. A woodcock was flushed from Wilderness Pond vegetation on 17 November that year and seven redshank flew north-east the very next day. Nearer to the present day, an oystercatcher flew north on 30 June 2005.

Female goosander

MANDARIN DUCK

Many newcomers to Christchurch Park are amazed when they see a drake mandarin for the first time, either on the Round or Wilderness Ponds. The first record of a mandarin here was of a drake on 7 September 1977. In spring drake mandarins are, let's face it, the most exotic of all duck. Their colours are wonderful, and the duck's design is unusual in that it has orange sails – large feathers that protrude above the drake's back. Moreover, the bird is so obliging. It seems to have no fear of onlookers and will swim quite close to the watching public. However, along with all this glamorous plumage, it has another trick up its sleeve, for the mandarin's display is as exotic as its appearance. We have previously thoroughly described the mandarin in *Portrait of a Park* but two points ought to be reiterated.

The mandarin is a wood duck, which means that it is quite happy to be on small ponds that are enclosed by woodland. When we carried out our count of mandarins two years ago during their annual moult, we were disappointed at the low number of birds. However, we had forgotten to look upwards. Despite going through their moult, several mandarins were clambering about in branches overhead. The Friends of Christchurch Park fixed specially designed mandarin duck boxes to some of the trees edging the Wilderness Pond and they have readily taken to them. When the ducklings hatch, the female calls them down to the water and one by one the youngsters drop out of the box, barely making a splash as they land by the female's side. At first we had success with quite a few youngsters surviving to adulthood but sadly that is no longer true. We have a serious problem, not with the usual predator suspects (such as squirrels, rats, birds of prey or corvids), but with large gulls.

The Park is now a hunting ground for herring gulls and, in particular, lesser black-backed gulls. In 2013 one female mandarin brought off 15 ducklings but within three days these large gulls had eaten them all. Mallard ducklings go the same way as do young moorhens and, surprisingly, the majority of Canada goslings. This problem, I am afraid, is here to stay because these all-devouring gulls that nest on Ipswich's rooftops are rapidly increasing in number. It is thought that this may well be due to the birds feeding on rubbish tips and piggeries, and there are many of the latter in East Suffolk. Waste food left on the streets and open spaces of the town is another contributing factor to their success.

The second interesting fact about mandarins is that the youngsters can take up to 18 months to attain adult plumage. This means that in spring you can see drake mandarins looking splendid with their sails alongside drake mandarins that appear to be in adult plumage but lacking the sails. From our observations, this does not mean that sub-adult males are unable to mate. Far from it, in fact, as some females choose these less gaudy drakes in preference to the more resplendent ones. A few years ago, the mandarins would fiercely defend their young ducklings and, in one case, unpaired males strove to protect ducklings, but with the ever increasing numbers of large gulls over the last couple of years, their defence has been rendered futile. Mandarin numbers have dropped and the build-up of moulting ducks in late summer is also now greatly reduced.

Wood duck are great travellers and extremely fast and agile flyers. We think that many mandarins have found more secure waterways in which to moult and indeed breed. We know that these colourful birds visit several parks in Ipswich and that breeding takes place on the ponds at Purdis Heath golf course. The large gulls do not breed in that vicinity but have been seen passing overhead – perhaps they do not notice the mandarin ducklings. A drake Carolina, an American wood duck, used to fly in with the mandarins but sadly it has not been seen for the last two years.

Mandarins with a single drake Carolina

SPARROWHAWK AND KESTREL

Sparrowhawk

Most people's first encounter with a sparrowhawk is seeing a flash of brown or grey, and a pile of feathers on a lawn with more feathers floating down from a tree or a post. If you are quick enough to glance up to that post, you may see the sparrowhawk's prey being held down by needle-sharp talons attached to long yellow legs that give the unfortunate songbird very little chance of escape. You may even see the predator's eyes – pale yellow with a stare that seems almost evil.

On four Sundays in July and August every year, the Friends of Christchurch Park promote brass band concerts by the Upper Arboretum's Arts and Crafts Shelter. Fine weather usually sees about 300 visitors relaxing to the music of Andrew Lloyd Webber, George Gershwin or even the Beatles. Dozing in the sunlight, with feet tapping to the music, very few look upwards. If they did, they might see an event which also happens here annually at around this time. This is when young sparrowhawks take to the wing and invariably circle together with their parents overhead. If it were not for the music then the air would be full of immature 'spars' calling to the adults. Young birds of prey can be very noisy.

Sparrowhawks have nested in Christchurch Park since about the mid-1990s and although one pair traditionally nests in the Wildlife Reserve it is thought highly probable that another pair has been breeding quite close to the Park, perhaps in one of the large gardens. It is known that a pair breeds in the Ipswich New Cemetery nearby. Sparrowhawks will use traditional nesting sites, sometimes using locations alternately, the nest being prepared well before eggs are laid. These birds of prey are comparatively late nesters coinciding, of course, with the maximum number of juvenile songbirds on which to feed their young. The Park's spars nest in a tall Scots pine and the bulky nest, made of strong twigs, is quite visible from under the tree. During spring however there is usually no sign that sparrowhawks are nesting here at all. The female will incubate the eggs towards the end of May and there is hardly any movement as she sits tightly on the nest. On the whole, bird of prey eggs are beautifully marked and have been eagerly sought after by egg collectors. Sparrowhawk eggs are especially attractive, being rounded, mostly white with blotches and spots of red and dark brown.

The male will bring food to his mate – small birds that he has already plucked so there will be no tell-tale feathers on the ground beneath the nest. His visit to the sitting female will be extremely brief – blink and you will miss him. When the eggs hatch it will be the male who continues to bring food for both the female and her young though when the chicks are old enough to be left for a while she will also join in the hunt for food. Growing chicks, often four but sometimes up to six in a clutch, need a great deal of plucked food and, as the female is larger than her mate, she can bring to the nest collared doves, stock doves, wood pigeons and occasionally woodpeckers of both species. Soon the branches of the tree and the ground below become splattered with faeces, feathers and discarded pieces of dead birds, quite different from when the female is incubating her eggs.

The ability of accipiters (hawks), particularly the larger females, to fly at almost reckless speed through quite densely packed wooded areas, is amazing. When the young are hungry and call, the parents will arrive quite suddenly with food, dashing through the branches on rounded wings with semi-plucked carcasses in their talons. The parent birds may arrive quietly but the young do not follow suit and are often very, very noisy. Providing food for growing youngsters takes a heavy toll on the surrounding bird population – at first finches, tits and other small birds. Spars are not discerning creatures and might well be the main reason why nuthatches in our Park are perilously close to extinction. Male sparrowhawks are very adept at catching songbirds on bird tables and birdfeeders. A nuthatch intent on eating peanuts stands no chance whatsoever against this predator.

When the breeding season is over in Christchurch Park one is more likely to see a sparrowhawk circling overhead. Its long tail, rounded wings and size mean that it cannot be mistaken for any other bird. Looking upwards can be rewarding in spring and autumn as sparrowhawks use thermals on migration. Of course a bird of prey wheeling overhead is likely to arouse the interest of the local crow population which means continual mobbing until the thermal carries the intruder away. Sparrowhawks are now well established around Ipswich although not everyone welcomes them. In the past, the enemy of the spar was the gamekeeper and it's clear that the combination of gamekeepers and the pesticide debacle of the 1950s and 60s almost wiped this bird out of existence in this area. The sparrowhawk has been slow in regaining its numbers, much slower than the kestrel (although kestrel numbers have recently plummeted). But for those of us who appreciate a superb and, let's face it, a very beautiful killing machine, the sparrowhawk is luckily holding its own. We are indeed fortunate to have this bird of prey in the middle of Ipswich.

A pair of kestrels

Kestrel

The kestrel, still known as the kestrel hawk in some parts of Suffolk, is not a hawk like the spar. It is a falcon. A falcon has dark eyes (sparrowhawk and goshawk eyes are pale yellow) and the wings of a falcon are pointed not rounded, and reach to the end of the bird's tail. Once common, this quite small falcon is mysteriously in decline and, unfortunately, no longer breeds in our Park. Perhaps the reason for this is obvious because the kestrel is not a bird that flashes across the Park snatching birds on the wing; in fact, it rarely takes birds. The kestrel's food consists of small rodents and beetles spotted by this falcon as it hovers above the ground. Surely everyone has seen the 'windhover'? This bird could often be seen hovering close to motorways, and many children must have been kept amused whilst travelling with their parents by playing I-spy – "I spy a hovering kestrel". But we no longer see kestrels hanging over the Park, wings fluttering with tails outspread. I fear it is doubtful whether there are sufficient mice or beetles to support a single kestrel, let alone a breeding pair.

We are saddened by the decline of the kestrel and have always considered it to be a harmless bird of prey just like the hobby falcon. Of course all birds of prey have hooked beaks and very sharp talons, but there is a vast difference in the hunting methods of the kestrel and the sparrowhawk. The kestrel hovers when seeking its food, dropping down silently onto an unsuspecting vole. The sparrowhawk's method of hunting on the other hand seems quite frantic. With great skill it will dash between branches and seize a bird, often plucking it before it is dead. Christchurch Park is all the poorer for the lack of kestrels. Despite its nature, let's hope that our spars do not go the same way.

PIGEONS OF THE PARK

Some members of the public appear to be oblivious to many of the birds in our Park, and yet I have heard people gasp in amazement at the sight of a magpie – yes, a magpie. "Aren't they pretty, and look at those lovely long tails" I hear. But they are crows, quite evil really. Mind you, it is good that people like magpies, for at least magpies are being noticed. Wood pigeons on the other hand, despite being really very attractive, are not commented upon. People ignore them. 'Woodies' are common in our Park; they are fat and often reluctant to fly despite loose dogs chasing around the grassy areas. However, look carefully at these birds – fat yes, but bold, and colourful and, let's face it, delightful to have around.

Well, that's my verdict on wood pigeons, though not everyone agrees. My farming friends hate wood pigeons, classing them as vermin and calling them 'winged rats'. How can this be? It is the farmers' fault really since it is they who grow oilseed rape. They plant the seed in autumn and by the middle of winter the young plants are well-established, just right for the hordes of wood pigeons that arrive here to gorge themselves on the succulent oilseed rape leaves.

To deter the tens of thousands of pigeons from eating their crops, farmers have three methods of defence. First of all there are the bird scarers positioned in the fields of rape that let off an explosion every ten minutes or so. The pigeons take flight but then settle down again. Another bang, and up (and then back down) go the pigeons. After a while, the birds cease to take much notice. A more recent innovation is the use of kites as artificial birds of prey. These are anchored in the rape field and, although the plastic harriers

A wood pigeon at nest

look real enough, once again the gorging pigeons become used to the toys. The third technique is the use of marksmen. The gunmen are camouflaged in a hide amongst the rape. Model pigeons strung up on wires attached to a stake whirr around and dead pigeons are placed amongst the tender rape plants. When pigeons are attracted to the decoys they are blasted with a shotgun. Does this make a difference to the pigeon population? Not really. The method is expensive; and the few pigeons shot make little impact on the tens of thousands of winged rats.

The wood pigeon isn't the gardener's favourite bird either. Pigeons can do so much damage, especially to young green vegetables. But I like them. They are really not flying rats and on hot summer days their 'cooing' certainly adds to the enjoyment of our Park.

Another common pigeon here is the stock dove. I like stock doves too. Most people do not notice the difference between this bird and the 'woodie'. They vary from the farmers' enemy by being smaller and having no white neck markings or white wing bars. Instead, two dark bars on the wings make the stock dove resemble the blue homing pigeon. Whereas the wood pigeon makes its nest in a bush or a tree, stock doves nest in holes in trees. When Mabel, the Park's resident tawny owl, is not in situ then stock doves can be seen eyeing up the gaping hole of her roost. Stock doves must get quite a surprise when Mabel has young down in the oak tree's trunk.

The third pigeon or dove is the collared dove, which has only been in this country since the mid-1950s. A native of temperate and subtropical Asia, this gentle bird is really quite attractive, being warm brown with a distinctive black half-collar. But it is the voice which is so disappointing, sounding as if the bird is moaning. Mind you, the stock dove's call is also repetitive and boring as well. Although now common in our Park, the collared dove prefers to build its frail nest of twigs in the neighbouring gardens. I should also mention the turtle dove. Even gentler than the collared dove, this lovely little pigeon has declined so much that you will not find it in Christchurch Park or indeed hardly anywhere else in Suffolk. Much fabled in poetry and song, everyone loves a turtle dove; a beautiful bird which is now going the way of so many of our Park birds such as spotted flycatcher, hawfinch, lesser spotted woodpecker and tree sparrow.

This brings me to yet another dove or pigeon, the feral pigeon. I used to keep pigeons. I had a mishmash of blue check, blue barred, red check and something hereabouts known as the mealy red pigeon. I kept these pigeons for a purpose. I wanted to study doves and pigeons, so I substituted my homing pigeons' eggs for those of wood pigeons, turtle and collared doves. My pigeons would hatch their eggs and I would have wild doves in captivity. Very naughty now, but not so in those days of my childhood when I could study these birds closely. Maybe this is why I am so attracted to pigeons.

However, the feral pigeons of Ipswich are even more of a mishmash. Some appear very dark in colour and these I used to know as 'London' pigeons. Amongst this lot is another type of feral pigeon which resembles a rock dove. Now, this is an interesting point. What is a rock dove? Rock doves originate from coastal areas, breeding in holes in cliffs and caves mainly on the west coast of Britain. As such we do not have rock doves here; however some years ago I studied pigeons breeding in a Martello tower on the Suffolk coast near to Shingle Street. The flock of pigeons living there, numbering up to 40, were all of the rock dove type – greyish blue with black bars on wings and with white rumps. I could not tell these Martello dwellers from rock doves and I suggested that these were indeed rock doves of a sort. But local experts discarded my suggestion. So what were these pigeons? Why not rock doves? These birds did not associate with feral pigeons – in fact there were no feral pigeons amongst this Martello flock. I told my tale to a pigeon fancier and he could not see why rock doves should not have found their way to the Suffolk coast. I like to think that they were indeed rock doves but who knows?

There is a vast chasm between the proud strutting wood pigeon, the inquisitive stock dove, the delicate collared dove and those '57 varieties' that flock to the roofs of central Ipswich and sometimes fly into our Park. Just lately, the feral lot has been sorted out by the local peregrine falcons, but numbers of these pigeons are unfortunately still rising.

MABEL, OUR TAWNY OWL

It is not unusual to see a posse of photographers below the Park's oak tree in which Mabel roosts, and it is also not unusual to see cameras with telescopic sights of huge proportions. One expects to see such an army of photographers at, say, a football match but under an old oak tree in which sits a tawny owl? This emphasises just how famous Mabel has become. Surely she is this country's most photographed wild owl? Such is her fame that her fans travel from great distances just to get a glimpse of her, and am I alone in thinking that more and more Park visitors talk to her? We talk to dogs and cats but passing the time of day with a tawny owl – how daft can we get?

Of course, Mabel is famous. She has been resident in that oak tree since at least September 2008 and no matter what the weather might be there she sits, sometimes with eyes wide open, looking down on inquisitive observers or moving her head around following the scampering dogs unleashed by their owners. Mabel surveys the world – her world. How long before we find Mabel on a postage stamp? Her story has been told and updated in both of the Friends of Christchurch Park's two previous *Portrait* books but, as yet, no one has come up with a reason as to why she sits in the open in full view of her admiring entourage.

The lovely thing about having a tawny owl on display is that people, especially children who have never seen an owl, can be introduced to the wonderful world of birdwatching. I doubt if there will ever be a more obliging wild owl. Knowing the dangers that owls face, for five years now I have been advising people to really enjoy Mabel, as one day she will be gone for good. Thousands of visitors have acquired a great amount of knowledge because of her, not just about Mabel, but also of our other British owls. I have spent hours looking up at Mabel and have heard so many comments from other Park goers. Several onlookers ask the same question: "is Mabel stuffed?" But my favourite comment was made by a small girl who, looking up at Mabel (whose eyes were closed), turned to her mother and said "If Mabel is asleep Mummy, then why doesn't she fall out of her tree?"

Because Mabel has been studied for so long now, we know a great deal about her. In the most part this is thanks to the aforementioned army of photographers and in particular to Paul Sherman who, two years ago, captured the most astonishing pictures not only of Mabel but also of her mate and three youngsters. As far as I know, Paul is the only person to have photographed the whole family. It is very unusual to see a family of tawny owls together but Paul captured them all in the same tree not far from the original roost. I believe this is also the only time that Mabel's mate has been identified and, seeing them together, it was easy to spot the difference between male and female tawnies.

There is much concern each spring when Mabel goes missing from her roost. For those in the know, Mabel's disappearance causes little angst: she is laying her eggs deep in the hollow trunk of the oak tree. How far down we do not know and no attempt has been made to discover the actual nest site in the tree for fear of disturbing Mabel and driving her away for good. When the first egg of the clutch is laid, Mabel will start incubating. For the next two and half months there will be no sign of her. She will sit tight on her eggs for just over 30 days before the first one hatches. Generally, owls and birds of prey will start incubating when the first egg is laid which means that in a clutch of four the

"Mabel and Youngster" Reg Snook 2010

first owlet will be several days old when the final egg hatches. During this time Mabel is fed by her mate. He must bring food at night for he has not been seen at the entrance hole during daylight hours. We know that the diet of this pair of owls is mainly rats. Pellets have revealed no sign of birds. It is known that tawny owls do take birds at night when the birds themselves are roosting but we have no evidence of this with our Christchurch Park pair. So rats appear to be their main source of food. Where do these owls catch these rodents? It seems obvious really. There are rats near our ponds, and also in the large gardens that surround so much of our Park. The Old Cemetery, Constitution Hill and the spinney in Corder Road are all within hunting distance. Having lived in this area for over 40 years, I have first-hand knowledge of the numbers of rats around here. Food, it seems, is plentiful.

Park goers miss Mabel during the incubation period and while she is supervising her growing youngsters, and are delighted when she reappears, usually in September, albeit looking slightly dishevelled because of the wear and tear of incubating and bringing up her youngsters. They are even more delighted when one or more of the owlets are spotted perched on one of the lower branches of the oak tree. Shortly after this stage, the family moves across the nearby path to a group of smaller trees where they remain for several days, being fed by both parents, before the whole family moves even further away. When the young are fully grown they disperse to find their own territories with sufficient food and no competition from other owls. Autumn sees Mabel return to the roost hole where she moults, and the whole cycle begins again.

WOODPECKERS

The lesser spotted woodpecker, the smallest of our woodpeckers, deserted our Park in the mid-1990s for reasons still unknown. This leaves us with just two woodpecker species – the great spotted and the green (pictured above and below). Whereas numbers of the lesser spotted woodpecker have gradually declined, this is not so with the other two: if anything our remaining woodpeckers are increasing in numbers. We are lucky in having large areas of grassland suitable for the green variety, with plenty of mature trees ideal for great spotted woodpeckers. Both of these woodpeckers are very vocal and often we hear them well before we see them.

The green woodpecker is an extraordinary bird. Its name suggests that you might expect it to be entirely associated with trees, however it spends much of its time on the ground, especially on the grassy areas towards the northern end of Christchurch Park. It eats ants and has an extremely long sticky tongue with which to locate them below ground. In our Park green woodpeckers can often be seen in the company of mistle thrushes and, perhaps surprisingly, from a distance it is difficult to distinguish between them. Both hold themselves upright and are approximately the same size. When the birds take to the wing, however, the green woodpecker is much more prominent. It flies with a very undulating flight and is indeed very colourful. The crown of its head is red and it has a black surround to its eye as well as a black moustache. The upper-wing coverts (small feathers that cover the bases of the longer wing feathers) and back are green, but the most diagnostic colouring is its yellow rump. And, of course, it has a voice, a loud descending 'laugh' that gives the woodpecker its country name of 'yaffle'.

Both of our woodpeckers nest in holes in trees. Naturally the green woodpecker, the larger of the two, excavates a bigger hole. Some trees are riddled with holes, and the time to observe woodpeckers is in late spring when the young are large enough to peer out of the nest hole because the adults are forever coming and going with food. Woodpeckers returning to the nest will alight on the tree trunk and the young will crane forward to receive their meals. When green woodpeckers have hungry youngsters, they tend to

Great spotted woodpecker

lose their inhibitions and can readily be watched from a safe distance.

The great spotted woodpecker has, in some circles, been blamed for the decline of the lesser spotted woodpecker. It is suggested that competition for nesting sites has resulted in the smaller bird being unable to find suitable areas in which to breed. The larger variety is indeed a very smart bird, sharply defined in black and white. The male has a red patch on its nape whereas the female lacks any red on its head. Beware though, for young spotted woodpeckers have a red crown. Both male and female have a wonderfully crimson patch under the tail. You will not find great spotted woodpeckers on the ground but in woodpecker areas you will almost certainly see them on bird feeders. They love peanuts. This woodpecker is noisy with a series of "tck" calls being the usual announcement that it is in the trees, though from November through to spring the male drums.

A great spotted woodpecker in flight

"SPOTTED FLYCATCHERS"

SPOTTED FLYCATCHER

When I was young, three summer migrants always gave me particular pleasure. I roamed Warren and Bixley Heaths, then an area of rough fields lined by established hedgerows of oaks, elms and mature shrubs such as hawthorn but now covered in supermarkets and houses. This habitat was where these migrants bred. Red-backed shrikes nested in the hawthorns, redstarts in holes in mature trees, and spotted flycatchers in trees bordering the roads. Redstarts are just about holding on around Ipswich but not so the shrikes.

That leaves the spotted flycatcher, and sadly very few remain. Traditional sites have been deserted and one of the Park's favourite summer visitors has now disappeared, probably forever. How long will it be before it too no longer returns to Suffolk at all?

This tiny bird was friendly, so confiding and ever-welcoming. Many of us remember spotted flycatchers nesting in our porches, amongst the creepers in our trellises, over our exterior doors and windows and even in or on top of bird boxes. Spotted flycatchers are quite late arrivals, usually turning up in Britain in early May. Two broods are raised before they depart for their winter quarters in Africa. As their name suggests, these small brown birds depend on winged insects for food and in Christchurch Park it was always a pleasure to watch a male bird dash across the grass, snatch an insect and return to its perch. What made these birds so enjoyable to watch was the fact that they were so accommodating. You could stand only a few metres away from the bird's favourite perch and watch as it searched the area, its tail moving almost excitedly, and then see it catch its prey. I have looked on as a spotted flycatcher sought insects near the Mansion in high summer. This particular bird was partial to butterflies and I watched as it caught peacock butterflies and skilfully de-winged them using only its beak. Gently, the peacock's wings floated down to the ground below. Of all the birds that have disappeared from Christchurch Park, the spotted flycatcher is the bird that I miss most. It is just a small brown bird with a streaky breast, but what a charming character.

Spotted flycatchers invariably used to nest in oak trees in the Park, hidden amongst the rough bark or in a knothole. Up to three pairs bred each summer until at least 2002. The last breeding pair noted in the Park was in 2007. Since then the only sighting has been of a presumed passage bird on 2 June 2011. When they bred, flycatchers were present in the Park from early May to late September or early October. August was the best month for impressive totals, when breeding birds and their young were joined by passage birds. The highest recorded was 20 on 20 August 1982.

The records reveal the overall decline of spotted flycatcher numbers in Christchurch Park:

1975	3 pairs
18.05.1976	1
20.08.1982	20+
01.10.1982	2
06.07.2002	2 – 3 pairs
17.08.2003	6+
24.08.2003	8+
29.07.2005	1 – 2 juveniles
18.08.2006	8+ including 3 juveniles
13.07.2007	2 (breeding?)
21.08.2007	4+
02.06.2011	1

TREECREEPER AND NUTHATCH

Walking through the Park, people can be heard saying things such as "have you seen Mabel?" or "aren't the mandarin ducks spectacular?" You never hear anyone praising treecreepers! Why? Because treecreepers are tiny, brown and quite secretive. The vast majority of visitors to our Park, even some birdwatchers, do not see them. But treecreepers are fascinating and one of the Park's most successful breeding birds.

The treecreeper is a small bird, no more than 12.5cms in length, mottled brown with a distinctive white supercilium (eye stripe). But look for the bill, long and down-curved, which is ideal in its hunt for bark-dwelling insects. The bird is so named because (of course) it creeps rather jerkily up – not down – trees. The nuthatch goes down. The small treecreeper has very sharp claws with which to climb trees, and, like a woodpecker, has really strong tail feathers. Treecreepers are active but it is the high-pitched call that is the give-away. When family parties are searching for insects together, they seem to get very excited and call repeatedly. Christchurch Park's treecreepers can be seen mainly in the Wildlife Reserve; watch them fly down to the bottom of a tree, work their way up the trunk and then repeat the process.

Treecreepers usually build their nests where there is a gap between the bark and the tree trunk. Many of the old trees in Christchurch Park provide suitable nesting sites. However, one reason for the expansion of this bird in our Park is the provision of bat boxes. In 2010, bat boxes were placed on several trees at about 4.5 metres from the ground. Each tree had a number of boxes radiating in a circle around the trunk meaning the Wildlife Reserve held about 30 boxes. Not only were the boxes ideal for bats, of which the Park has at least five species, but they were perfect for treecreepers. There are, to be sure, more treecreepers using bat boxes than bats.

Young treecreepers leave the nest and crawl up the trunk of the host tree before huddling together to wait for their parents to feed them. The coloration of the young makes it very difficult for predators to spot them and when they leave the nest they are well-camouflaged against the bark of the tree. Credit is due to our local photographer Paul Sherman who has taken wonderful photographs of young treecreepers leaving the nest and then, as family groups, huddling together. It took much patience and a lot of skill to photograph these otherwise somewhat overlooked birds.

Ironically, the bird that often appears on the same page of bird books as the treecreeper, the colourful nuthatch, has had completely contrasting fortunes in the past few years. There was a time when nuthatches could be located in at least three areas of the Park. Sadly, the nuthatch now breeds in only one spot – quite close to Christchurch Mansion. We know from Paul Sherman's observations that young nuthatches fledge but they never seem to reach adulthood: immature birds are never seen. Now numbers are down to a single pair. The year 2014 is crucial for the Park's nuthatches – we might be losing them altogether. The decline does not appear to be due to lack of food or habitat for this species loves our ancient oak trees (of which we have many) and there are plenty of suitable holes for nesting.

Sparrowhawks may lie behind the nuthatch's decline here. Several people living in the houses whose gardens back on to the Park encourage birds by the use of bird feeders. Nuthatches are attracted to peanuts and sparrowhawks are attracted to nuthatches. Therefore nuthatches on bird feeders are easy pickings for this bird of prey. Whereas treecreeper numbers are increasing, the nuthatch faces extinction in our Park. Perhaps this reveals the importance of camouflage. If your plumage is blue and orange as opposed to brown then it is much more likely you will become prey to a 'spar'.

A male sparrowhawk swoops through the Wildlife Reserve – after a nuthatch?

THE CROW FAMILY

Apart from the large gulls that terrorise wildfowl on the Wilderness and Round Ponds, perhaps the most noticeable birds of Christchurch Park are the crows. Magpies, of course, attract attention; they are, in a crow sort of way, quite glamorous as well as being very tame. Many people who are unaware of the magpie's traditionally evil reputation are delighted to see this crow. It is not just black and white as first appearance suggests. In certain lights the magpie has a dazzling set of feathers with iridescent colours of mauve, blue, green and orange/brown. The magpie struts across the grassy areas near the Mansion knowing full well that he is a resplendent master criminal. This long-tailed crow is safe in our Park. No one will shoot him and there will always be food available, from pieces of sandwich, bits of take-away meals and the eggs and young of smaller birds. No wonder the magpie is increasing in numbers. He is a survivor and a chancer. Watch him and watch his mind working. He cannot be outwitted.

Everybody knows the black corvid of our Park, the carrion crow. Or do we? Park visitors are sometimes quite ignorant of our resident birds but you would feel that most people would recognise a crow. Sadly, that is just not the case. Crows are confused with jackdaws, rooks and, believe it or not, even magpies despite being all black: black feathers, black beak, black legs and black eyes. It should not really be confused with any other species of crow. Jackdaws are smaller with grey mantle and head. Magpies are pied and we do not have hooded crows here. I think that crows don't like magpies, especially in the breeding season. Likewise, not many birds appreciate crows. Our Park crows are clever and sometimes amusing. They thrive in our neighbourhood, being able to find food in our Park and in the surrounding gardens. They search these gardens for household scraps and, after having their fill, will bury the remainder – inevitably being unable to locate it again (well, at least not in my garden!). The crows that nest (in very tall trees) in the Park and in the local gardens fare extremely well and many young are fledged. I would suggest that the numbers of crows in Christchurch Park will remain high; they have few enemies, they are not culled and there is ample food. Like magpies and the large gulls, they are great scavengers.

There are many very old trees in the Park – oaks, limes, horse and sweet chestnuts. They contain holes which are very suitable for jackdaws to build their nests. But there is still considerable competition for these nest sites. Tawny owls and grey squirrels will easily oust jackdaws and many other holes are used by nesting stock doves. Luckily for the Park's jackdaw population, many of the large houses adjacent to the Park have disused chimneys which jackdaws have taken to use for breeding purposes, sometimes in groups of several pairs. Nesting material is gathered from the Park, taken to the chimneys and dropped down the holes to form a platform. When the young are fledged the birds stick together and can be seen flying around the neighbourhood, the air full of jackdaws calling their name. No wonder a flock of jackdaws is called a 'clattering'.

Rooks are no longer seen anywhere near the town centre. As we have said, the Park's rookery in the tall horse chestnut trees near to the Bethesda Baptist Church has been deserted since 1978. Therefore the only other crow to be found in Christchurch Park is the jay. This is a beautifully-coloured but at the same time an aggressive and noisy bird. Often the harsh call of the jay is the first sign that this crow is around. Quite elusive during the breeding season, jays become extremely prominent in autumn when family parties search the ground for acorns beneath the Park's oak trees. Unlike magpies and carrion crows, the jay nests much lower down, often only about 2.5 metres from the ground. Again, unlike the larger crows, jays build a nest of small twigs and grass which resembles closely that of a blackbird's nest. The eggs too are similar to those of a blackbird being, for such a large bird, comparatively small. As I have said, other members of the crow family – raven, chough, rook, carrion and hooded crow, jackdaw and magpie are basically black. The jay, however, is magnificently coloured. In fact it could be described as a stunning bird and, in times past, the jay's wing feathers of blue, black and white were well sought after for decorating hats. Like other members of its family, jays are notorious for taking eggs and the young of songbirds. In fact the jay does more harm to nesting songbirds than any other corvid, and that includes the magpie. This is because it lives right amongst its prey and is familiar with the bird life of hedgerows and woods. The jay is a pretty, but also a pretty deadly bird.

Fieldfare

WINTER AND SUMMER VISITORS

Winter visitors

Two Scandinavian thrushes, redwing and fieldfare, are regular winter visitors, especially in October and November when they first arrive in Britain. At the end of winter, redwings again feature as they search for food to enable them to build up sufficient fat supplies and energy levels to fuel their flight back across the North Sea and onwards to their breeding grounds in the northern regions.

The earliest fieldfare to be recorded in the autumn was on 7 September 1981 but the Park's peak day total was of 160 flying west on 14 November 2005. Redwings are occasionally noted in September but the peak day totals occur later, for example, 350 flying west on 8 October 1975 and 150 flying west on 2 November 2006. Impressive counts of ground-feeding redwings have been made in winter, for example, 175 on 27 January 1977 and 100 on 6 March 2010. A group of 100 redwings on 8 February 1978 included a creamy, buff-coloured individual. Fortunately for the bird involved, there were no sparrowhawks in the Park at that time!

A late redwing was in the Park between 5 and 12 May 1976. Even more remarkable was a redwing with a damaged left wing which frequented the shrubbery around the Wilderness Pond between 17 May and 9 September 1977. This was the first recorded instance of over-summering by the species in Suffolk.

Several gardens surrounding the Park record mid-winter blackcaps. Such records for the Park include a singing male in February and March 1977 and a male and female together in January 1978. The birds are almost certainly as much winter visitors as our fieldfares and redwings. They will have bred in central Europe and then migrated west to take advantage of Britain's relatively mild, winter climate.

The siskin is a winter visiting finch from Scandinavia and northern Britain. It is a small streaky-yellow, black and green finch, which specialises in extracting seeds from the cones of the Park's alder trees. They are not easy to count in the tops of the alders, but several sightings of between 20 and 30 have been recorded over the years. A late male was noted on 1 June 1977.

Another primarily winter visiting finch that could often be seen with the siskins in the alder trees was the lesser redpoll. Although as many as 40 were present in the winters of the 1970s and early 1980s, this small streaky-black, brown and grey finch with red on the forehead has declined sharply as a breeding species in eastern England in recent years. This has been reflected in the Park's wintering population, which now rarely numbers more than one or two.

Summer visitors

As well as being winter visitors, moving back to central Europe to breed in the spring, blackcaps are also summer visitors to the Park. These summer birds over-winter in southern Europe and northern Africa and arrive back in the Park from late March onwards into early May. Up to five singing males have been recorded in the Park. Let's hope they all bred.

Another summer visiting warbler is the chiffchaff, a small brown bird with a distinctive "chiff-chaff, chiff-chaff" song. It seems likely that at least two pairs breed each summer –

one in the area of the Wilderness Pond and another in the north-west corner of the Park.

A long-distance migrant warbler that is a fairly regular summer visitor is the lesser whitethroat, a very smart grey, white and brown bird. In most springs we record at least one singing male, and in the late 1970s this species almost certainly bred in the Park. One or two are located in autumn before they commence their migration south-eastwards across southern Europe and then south to Uganda and Kenya in eastern Africa.

Willow warblers are very similar to chiffchaffs but are more yellow in colour and with a completely different song. This species is declining rapidly in southern and eastern England. In the 1970s and 80s one or two spring migrants would occur in the Park although breeding was never suspected. In the autumn, immature willow warblers (probably from the Scandinavian breeding population) would occur regularly between late July and mid-September with a peak day total of eight individual birds.

This warbler over-winters in western Africa south of the Sahara desert. Nowadays, spring migrants are not recorded in the Park and only one or two are seen in late summer, mainly in August.

SCARCE VISITORS

Although most birdwatching in the Park involves common birds, as with any site that is watched regularly, scarcer species inevitably occur from time to time, particularly in the autumn.

The hobby, a summer visiting falcon from central tropical Africa which feeds on dragonflies, swallows, martins and swifts, is increasing as a breeding species in England. As such it is surprising that there is only one record from the Park which occurred on 4 June 2004.

The cuckoo is declining rapidly in England. There were several records in the Park in the 1970s including one which remained in the vicinity of Snow Hill between 12 and 23 August 1975. The only relatively recent occurrence was on 15 May 2004.

An intriguing sight was that of a short-eared owl, probably of Continental/Scandinavian origin, being mobbed by crows over the Park on 8 November 2011. Much rarer was an alpine swift from southern Europe in late August 2012.

Sand martins are abundant summer visitors to Britain from western and central Africa but there are only six records for the Park mainly in early autumn when they are on southerly autumn migration. Yellow wagtails are also summer visitors to Britain but they are also declining rapidly: only four have been noted and these were flying over the Park. Grey wagtails, however, are both resident and winter visitors to our part of Britain. During most winters one is noted regularly in the centre of Ipswich so it is somewhat surprising that until recently there have been relatively few sightings in the Park. Tree pipits are closely related to meadow pipits but, unlike that species which are resident birds, tree pipits are summer visitors to Britain from tropical Africa. They are rapidly declining in Suffolk and there have been only two records in the Park, both in August, when they would have been on their southerly autumn migration.

Waxwings are spectacular, irruptive visitors from Scandinavia. If they have had a successful breeding season in the north of Europe but the berry crop fails there, then they move south-westwards across western Europe. There was such an irruption in 2004 and some visited the Park with up to 75 present in early December.

Reed warblers are common summer visitors from western Africa to Suffolk's plentiful reed beds; although such habitat does not exist in the Park at least six are known to have occurred here, including two singing in late May/early June in the Wilderness Pond's vegetation. Wood warblers breed principally in northern and western areas of Britain having over-wintered in western Africa but the breeding population is declining rapidly. There have been at least eight sightings in the Park involving three in the spring and five in the autumn – these latter birds are likely to have bred, or been bred, in Scandinavia.

Other warblers to have been noted in the Park include two autumn common whitethroats (heading back to the Sahara) and five garden warblers, of which four were in July/August as they also migrated back to western Africa.

Pied flycatchers are immaculate birds which breed in western and northern Britain having over-wintered in western Africa. To the best of our knowledge, there has never been a spring migrant pied flycatcher in the Park. However, in late summer, birds from the Scandinavian breeding population arrive on the east coast of Britain usually after east/north-east winds. Pied flycatchers were noted regularly in the Park each autumn until 2005 with a maximum of six on 18 August 1977 and 25 August 1984. Unfortunately, as with so many passerines of west African origin, populations have been declining in recent years. As such, it seems likely that pied flycatchers will be only erratic visitors to the Park in the foreseeable future.

Undoubtedly the most spectacular bird to be recorded in the Park has been the singing male golden oriole present in mid-May 2013. In recent years, the only location to support breeding golden orioles in Britain was Lakenheath Fen in west Suffolk but it would appear that the golden oriole is no longer a British-breeding bird. Golden orioles over-winter in sub-Saharan Africa and it seems likely that the Park bird was an over-shooting individual from the Continent.

With their 'bronzy' shoulders, vivid green upper parts and striking black and white head pattern, firecrests are often described by birders as 'little jewels'. They are closely related to goldcrests (hybridisation has occurred) and are just as small – they are the joint smallest of the British bird. Firecrests have a varied status in Britain – being spring migrants, autumn migrants, winter visitors and scarce breeders. The principal record in the Park involved one with food in its beak in July 1988. Hopefully this bird was breeding locally. At least six others have been noted in the Park including a singing male between 18 and 26 April 1978.

Marsh tits are highly sedentary British birds. They rarely move far from their nesting sites and do not breed in the Park so the sight of one in the Lower Arboretum on 15 September 1977 was totally unexpected. As their name suggests, reed buntings are associated with Suffolk's reed beds and movements are generally noted in mid-winter as they search for food in harsh weather. This is probably the reason for the Park's sole record on 19 January 1978.

As with waxwings, common crossbills are occasionally irruptive visitors to Britain from the Continent as well as being scarce residents especially in Suffolk's Breckland. These bulky finches irrupt when their food, in the form of pine seeds, becomes scarce. Irruptions between October 2011 and May 2012 witnessed at least 10 flying west over the Park with a maximum of five on 23 February 2012.

Mention should also be made of three members of the thrush/chat family which have been seen in the Park just once. A female wheatear was present on the open grass area on 21 April 2006. This species is a trans-Saharan migrant and the first birds usually arrive back in Britain in late February or early March. Given the date, it seems likely that our bird was heading for breeding grounds well north of Britain – perhaps even Greenland. The majority of black redstarts over-winter in France, Spain or northern Africa but they are amongst the earliest spring migrants to return to Britain, and an individual was reported on Snow Hill on 6 March 1978. They generally nest at industrial sites so hopefully this bird was on its way to a Suffolk breeding location. The ring ouzel is closely related to the blackbird and nests on mountainous regions of northern Britain and Europe. They over-winter in southern Europe and northern Africa and stop off in Suffolk on their way northwards, hence the occurrence on Snow Hill on 28 April 1975.

BIRDS FLYING OVER THE PARK

Autumn is an exciting time for bird migration over the Park. In the chapter on winter and summer visitors, reference has been made to the large movements of fieldfares and redwings in the autumn. However, several additional species have been noted moving over the Park, sometimes involving birds of Continental origin moving west towards milder areas.

Skylarks, meadow pipits and yellowhammers are more typically associated with Suffolk's farmland and heathland. However, during September and October, skylarks and meadow pipits have regularly been noted moving over the Park, principally in the early mornings. The maximum day totals have been five skylarks and sixteen meadow pipits.

Movements of yellowhammers have been more irregular with sightings in seven months and a maximum day total of four. These latter birds were heading north-east on 22 February 1978 so may have been returning to the Continent.

Swallows and house martins do not breed in the Park. Although generally regarded as summer visitors to Britain, they are only noted in appreciable totals over the Park as they migrate south in September and early October. For example, 60 house martins on 14 September 2005, 50 swallows on 29 September 1981 and 25 house martins on 12 October 1976. A very late house martin was present over the Lower Arboretum on 11 November 1978.

Swifts are the ultimate summer visitors to Britain, generally being present for a hectic breeding season between early May and early August. This species does not breed in the Park but birds from local breeding sites are regularly seen feeding over it. An exceptionally late individual was noted over the Upper Arboretum on 6 November 1974.

Common terns are more generally noted as summer visitors to our estuaries, reservoirs and lakes but singles were recorded flying over the Park on 30 August 1979 and 5 July 2005.

Brent geese are winter visitors from Russia to Suffolk's coast and estuaries but they do occasionally wander inland. However, the intended destination of 20 brent geese flying north over the Park on 8 November 1975 and 13 flying north on 29 November 1978 is anybody's guess!

The common buzzard is one of Suffolk's more recent ornithological success stories having returned to breed in the county in 1999 after an absence of 125 years. The species bred at up to 10 sites in Suffolk in 2012 but has not yet done so in the Park. However, common buzzards have been seen passing over the Park each year since 2008 with a peak of three on 11 March 2011.

On 6 May 2014 a new bird was added to the Park's list – a honey buzzard was seen flying overhead. Thousands of honey buzzards spend the winter in tropical Africa before migrating up through Europe in the spring to breed, mainly in forests, the nest usually being in a tall tree. A few pairs breed in Britain but this bird was probably on its way to northern Europe.

On the morning of 31 May 2014 a raven was seen flying north over the Park being mobbed by 11 jackdaws. Ravens are gradually spreading throughout Suffolk but this was again a first record for the Park.

"BLACK ON BLACK" JACKDAWS MOBBING A RAVEN

WHAT OF THE FUTURE?

We have documented some of the many changes that have taken place in the avifauna of Christchurch Park over the last 50 years, but what of the next half-century?

The massive reductions in the numbers of passerines that were regularly noted in the 1970s and 1980s are now generally considered to be linked to climate change. Birds are struggling to synchronise their breeding with the availability of food for their young and we can only assume that this situation will gradually worsen.

Some additional species might possibly become regular breeders here in the not-too-distant future. Cormorants have been regular visitors to the Wilderness Pond in the autumn and winter months since 2005. Now they can be seen sitting high up in the trees around the pond – could these trees be potential nesting sites? Cormorants have only nested in Suffolk in recent times since 1998, at Loompit Lake, Trimley St Martin, where up to 100 pairs nest in trees – very encouraging if you like cormorants.

It seems that over recent years cormorants' feeding habits have changed. No longer are these voracious fish eaters confined to the sea and rivers. Instead they actively seek out lakes and ponds such as ours for fresh supplies of fish on which to feast. Whereas perhaps it matters little if the Park's fish are eaten, the problem arises when cormorants visit those lakes commercially stocked with trout and carp. Herons no longer have sole fishing rights on inland waterways. Although cormorants are a protected species, anglers are so annoyed with seeing these more expert hunters catching and eating what they see as the angler's quarry that cormorants are being illegally shot. Those Park visitors who do not like seeing our splendid goldfish disappearing down a cormorant's throat may have to look the other way. But controlling cormorants and, for that matter lesser black-backed gulls, is much easier said than done.

As we have said, another relatively recent addition to the list of Suffolk's breeding birds is the summer visiting hobby. This bird of prey has been a rare visitor to the Park but is increasing dramatically elsewhere in Suffolk to the extent that we can surely look forward to regular sightings in the not-too-distant future. If that does happen, then hobbies might look for a site in which to breed in the Park. The Wildlife Reserve is the obvious choice but whether this site's breeding sparrowhawks would be prepared to tolerate these small falcons is another matter. However, as hobbies prefer to breed in the old nests of carrion crows, there would surely be no shortage of potential sites.

An excellent, but perhaps unlikely proposal, would be to have a large protected area of scrub available in the Park which might, just might, attract a pair of common whitethroats and, who knows, even a pair of nightingales – dream on!

Although strictly outside of this book's time constraints, it is known that two pairs of wrynecks bred in the Park way back in 1948 – the trees in which they bred are probably still standing. It is not outside the realms of possibility that a spring or autumn wryneck could occur in the Park. What a challenge for today's birdwatchers! In the autumn of 2013, there was a fall of wrynecks on the east coast with one recorded in a garden in Manor Road, just a few hundred metres from Christchurch Park.

Will we ever see nightingales nesting in our Park?

Even more likely for tomorrow's birdwatchers are sightings overhead of peregrines, red kites, common buzzards, little egrets and even ravens as these species gradually, or in some cases rapidly, increase in Suffolk.

There is little doubt that carrion crows and magpies will continue to increase in numbers. They are both social birds within their species and, unless there is a (highly unlikely) cull, then numbers will most probably continue to grow. Scavenging is one of the reasons for these birds' success and we cannot see the feeding habits of homo sapiens changing. Our Park encourages visitors with a whole range of events which attract thousands of people. Thousands of people means tonnes of litter and amongst that litter will always be waste food for corvids and large gulls.

Much has been written here and in the two previous books in the Christchurch Park trilogy on large gulls. The 'invasion' of herring and, especially, lesser black-backed gulls over southern English towns such as Ipswich, has been, in ornithological terms, nothing short of amazing. If crows are great scavengers then these gulls are super scavengers. Fearless where food and nesting sites are concerned, these birds will continue to increase in number. Once again, there are no predators to control them. What sort of predator would tackle the Ipswich gulls? It would take councils getting so fed up with the mess and the noise together with residents' fear of gulls before any action might be taken. The cost would be huge and anyway how on earth could you really start reducing numbers of lesser black-backed gulls? Shooting? Trapping? Preventing the gulls from nesting? It is probably just not feasible.

Perhaps some readers may think us over-pessimistic in relation to the birds that we have lost, not only in

Christchurch Park but also in Suffolk as a whole. We have tried to explain the state of birdlife in our Park today in relation to the years gone by. Unfortunately we believe that we are justified in our pessimism and, yes, we are right to be worried about the future of many of our songbirds. We are also concerned about the ascendance of what we term 'predator' species – crows, large gulls and cormorants. There will surely come a time when numbers of these birds will reach saturation point, but how can our wildfowl population continue to lose all their young to them? How long before the cormorants will have fished all they can from our ponds? Should certain species be offered protection? Should we even consider a selective cull of some others?

Fifty years ago these predator species were controlled by gamekeepers. Gibbets were decorated with crows, sparrowhawks, tawny owls and even hedgehogs. Some suggest that, as far as our songbirds were concerned, gamekeepers did a good job but did they really?

Fortunately in my opinion such gamekeepers and their 'dark arts' no longer have a place in our countryside. Control of predator species by shooting, trapping or even poisoning is simply neither feasible nor desirable in Christchurch Park. But if this is to be the case, is there an answer to the loss of our songbirds? Habitats have changed drastically too and, together with the increasing number of visitors, our Park has become quite a challenging place for birdlife, especially in the breeding season. Perhaps if we can improve certain habitats in the Park then songbird numbers may increase.

However, as a race, we humans have become extravagantly wasteful. We discard huge amounts of food and litter it everywhere. Even much of our household rubbish, that finishes up on landfill sites, contains food – ideal for large scavenging gulls and crows. A typical large-gull incident occurred in Ipswich at the end of April 2014. On the ground outside a busy fast food emporium was a lesser black-backed gull with a half-eaten bacon sandwich between its mandibles. Afraid? Not this bird. Above the bacon buttie shop was the gull's mate sitting on eggs. This was not an isolated incident. In fact, it is typical of the large gulls' brilliant ability to adapt to our wasteful way of life. In August, as parent birds desperately search for food for their now-fledged youngsters, lesser black-backed gulls become even more fearless particularly in Arras Square in the centre of Ipswich and by the bus station.

Almost all our waterfowl youngsters suffer from the predation of large gulls. The ducklings and goslings provide easy pickings for them but it is very dispiriting that mallard, mandarin, moorhen and Canada geese lose most of their young. It is also disappointing and often upsetting for the many Park visitors who are unacquainted with the eating habits of these scavenging gulls. A few Canada goslings survive because of fierce defence by the adults, but Canada geese are also not everyone's cup of tea.

In this book we have been somewhat agents of doom concerning the loss of so many of the Park's passerines, and quite rightly so, but one bird, one gloriously attractive little bird, has bucked the trend. This, of course, is the delightful goldfinch. Numbers of this beautiful finch have soared. Can there be a more welcoming sight than that of a goldfinch, or even two or three goldfinches, singing from atop a television aerial? This is now a very common sight but it is difficult to explain the reasons for the increase. Is it the availability of food? Many gardens adjacent to our Park have bird tables with feeders containing niger seed and sunflower hearts. Could it be the availability of nesting sites? The nearby large gardens are also full of ornamental shrubs, fruit and other trees. Probably it is a combination of both these factors but, whatever the reason, how wonderful that one bird, one small beautiful songster, is doing so well. Would that this were the case for so many others of our songbirds.

We have proved, or rather the goldfinch has proved, that if the habitat is right and if there is enough food available, bird numbers can increase. We have stated the facts regarding the birds of Christchurch Park but let us be cheerful. If a captive-breeding programme in the West Country can revitalise the fortunes of the cirl bunting, then perhaps a similar breeding and release programme in areas of Suffolk can help other threatened species.

The next few years will be decisive for Christchurch Park's birds. One thing is certain; we shall need more enthusiastic recorders and observers in our Park. Just two or three people have supplied the bulk of the sightings in this book. We appeal to all visitors to Christchurch Park to record their sightings using the recording facilities in the Reg Driver Visitor Centre. The observations of dozens of observers would soon no doubt encourage the publication of a whole new book about the wonderful birds of Christchurch Park.

LIST OF BIRDS OBSERVED IN OR SEEN FLYING OVER THE PARK

Below is a list of the bird species recorded in, or flying over, Christchurch Park during the last 50 years. We have divided it into two sections: those birds that you have a good chance of seeing (weather, season and good fortune permitting) and those that have been seen in the Park but which you may have to be particularly lucky to spot. It is formatted according to accepted ornithological practice and has been compiled by Philip Murphy from his own observations and those of other reputable ornithologists. Ornamental pinioned waterfowl are not included.

Birds you have a good chance of seeing here

Mute swan
Canada goose
Mandarin
Mallard
Cormorant
Grey heron
Sparrowhawk
Moorhen
Black-headed gull
Common gull
Lesser black-backed gull
Herring gull
Feral pigeon
Stock dove
Wood pigeon
Collared dove
Tawny owl
Swift
Kingfisher

Green woodpecker
Great spotted woodpecker
Swallow
House martin
Pied wagtail
Wren
Dunnock
Robin
Blackbird
Fieldfare
Song thrush
Redwing
Mistle thrush
Blackcap
Chiffchaff
Goldcrest
Long-tailed tit
Blue tit
Great tit

Coal tit
Nuthatch
Treecreeper
Jay
Magpie
Jackdaw
Carrion crow
Starling

House sparrow
Chaffinch
Greenfinch
Goldfinch
Siskin
Linnet
Lesser redpoll

Other birds that have been seen here

Greylag goose
Brent goose
Great black-backed gull
Shelduck
Carolina (Wood duck)
Shoveler
Teal
Tufted duck
Goosander
Pheasant
Little grebe
Common buzzard
Honey buzzard
Peregrine falcon
Kestrel
Hobby
Oystercatcher
Golden plover
Lapwing
Common snipe
Woodcock
Whimbrel
Redshank
Common sandpiper

Common tern
Turtle dove
Cuckoo
Short-eared owl
Alpine swift
Wryneck
Lesser spotted woodpecker
Skylark
Sand martin
Meadow pipit
Tree pipit
Yellow wagtail
Grey wagtail
Waxwing
Black redstart
Wheatear
Ring ouzel
Sedge warbler
Reed warbler
Garden warbler
Lesser whitethroat
Common whitethroat
Wood warbler
Willow warbler

Firecrest
Spotted flycatcher
Pied flycatcher
Marsh tit
Rook
Raven
Golden oriole
Tree sparrow
Brambling
Common crossbill
Bullfinch
Hawfinch
Yellowhammer
Reed bunting

A lesser white-fronted goose has been sighted in the Park but it was probably an escapee from a wildfowl collection.

WILDLIFE INDEX

Numbers in bold indicate an illustration.

Alder, 15, 52
Alpine swift, 54, 69
Ants, 39
Ash, **14**

Bats, 45-46
Beetles, 29
Black-backed gull, 5-6, 17-18, **18**, 20, 23, 62, 64, 66, 68. *See also* Gull
Blackbird, 10, 12, 50, 57, 68
Blackcap, 51-52, 68
Black-headed gull, 20, 68. *See also* Gull
Black redstart, 43, 57, 69
Blue tit, 10, 68
Brambling, 15, 70
Brent goose, 59, 69
Bullfinch, 13, **14**, 70
Butterfly, 44

Canada goose, 19, 23, 66, 68
Carolina duck, 20, 24, **24**, 69
Carrion crow, *see* Crow
Cats, 9, 10, 35
Chaffinch, 15, 69
Chestnut trees, 5, 6, 15-16, 49. *See also individual species*
Chiffchaff, 52-53, 68
Chough, 50
Cirl bunting, 67
Coal tit, 69
Collared dove, 26, 32-34, 68
Common buzzard, 59, **59**, 64, 69
Common crossbill, 57, 70
Common gull, 68. *See also* Gull
Common sandpiper, 21, 69

Common snipe, 21, 69
Common tern, 59, 69
Common whitethroat, 55, 62, 69
Cormorant, 5-6, **6**, 61-62, 65, 68
Crow, **iv**, 6, 12, 15-16, 27, 30, 48-50, 54, 62, 64, 65-66, 69
Cuckoo, 54, **54**, 69

Dogs, 10, 30, 35
Dove, *see individual species*
Dragonfly, 54
Duck, 5-6, 17, 23, 66. *See also individual species*
Dunnock, 10, 68

Elm, 43

Feral cat, *see* Cats
Feral pigeon, 33-34, 68
Fieldfare, **50**, 51, 52, 58, 68
Finch, 27, 52, 57. *See also individual species*
Firecrest, 56, 70
Fish, 5, 61. *See also* Goldfish

Garden warbler, 55, 69
Goldcrest, 56, 68
Golden oriole, 56, 70
Golden plover, 21, 69
Goldfinch, 66-67, 69
Goldfish, 5, **6**, 62. *See also* Fish
Goosander, 20, **21**, 69
Goose, 17, 19, 66. *See also individual species*
Goshawk, 29
Great black-backed gull, 69

Great spotted woodpecker, 39-41, **41**, 68. *See also* Woodpecker
Great tit, 10, 68
Greenfinch, 69
Green woodpecker, 12, 39-41, **39**, 68. *See also* Woodpecker
Grey heron, *see* Heron
Greylag goose, 19, 69
Grey squirrel, 9, 12, 22, 49
Grey wagtail, 54-55, 69
Gull, 9, 17-18, 20, 22-24, 48, 49, 64-66. *See also individual species*

Hawfinch, 13, 33, 70
Hawthorn, 43
Hedgehog, 65
Heron, 20, 61, 68
Herring gull, 17-18, 23, 64, 68. *See also* Gull
Hobby, 29, 54, 62, 69
Holm oak, 17
Homing pigeon, 32, 33
Honey buzzard, 59, 69
Hooded crow, 48, 50
Horse chestnut, 6, 15-16, 49. *See also* Chestnut
House martin, 54, 58, 68
House sparrow. *See* Sparrow

Insects, 9, 43-44, 45

Jackdaw, 16, 48-50, 60, **60**, 69
Jay, 12, 49-50, 69

Kestrel, 25, 27, **28**, 29, 69
Kingfisher, 20, 68

Lapwing, 21, 69
Lesser black-backed gull, *see* Black-backed gull, *also* Gull

Lesser redpoll,13, 52, 69
Lesser spotted woodpecker, 13, 33, 39, 69. *See also* Woodpecker
Lesser white-fronted goose, 19, 70
Lesser whitethroat, 53, 69
Lime tree, 49
Linnet, 13, 69
Little egret, 64
Little grebe, 20, 69
Long-tailed tit, 68

Mabel, *see* Tawny owl
Magpie, 12, **16**, 17, 30, 48-50, 64, 69
Mallard, 19, 23, 66, 68
Mandarin duck, 6, 9, 17, 22-24, **24**, 45, 66, 68
Marsh Tit, 57, 70
Meadow pipit, 55, 58, 69
Mice, 29
Mistle thrush, 10, 11, **11**, 12, 39-40, 68. *See also* Thrush
Moorhen, 17, 19, 23, 66, 68
Muscovy duck, 20
Mute swan, 19, 68

Nightingale, 62, **63**
Nuthatch, 9, 27, 45-47, 69

Oak, 5, 32, 35, 36, 38, 43, 44, 46, 49, 50
Oilseed rape, 30, 32
Ostrich, **3**
Oystercatcher, 21, 69

Palm-nut vulture, 1
Peacock butterfly, 44
Peregrine falcon, 34, 69
Pheasant, 69
Pied flycatcher, 56, 70

Pied wagtail, 68
Pigeon, 30-34. *See also individual species*
Pine, 7, 26, 57

Rat, 20, 29, 30, 32, 38
Raven, **vi**, 1, 6-7, 50, 60, **60**, 64, 70
Red-backed shrike, 9, 43
Red kite, 64
Redshank, 21, 69
Redstart, *see* Black redstart
Redwing, 51, 52, 58, 68
Reed beds, 55, 57
Reed bunting, 57, 70
Reed warbler, 55, 69
Rhododendron, 12
Ring ouzel, 57, 69
Roach, 5
Robin, 10, 68
Rock dove, 33-34
Rook, 6, **7**, 15-16, 48-50, 70

Sand martin, 54, 69
Scots pine, *see* Pine
Sedge warbler, 69
Shelduck, 20, 69
Short-eared owl, **iv**, 54, 69
Shoveler, 20, 69
Siskin, 15, 52, 69
Skylark, 58, 69
Song thrush, 12, 68. *See also* Thrush
Sparrow, 1, 13, 33, 69, 70
Sparrowhawk, 9, 17, 25-29, 46-47, **47**, 51, 62, 65, 68
Spotted flycatcher, 9, 33, **42**, 43-44, 70
Squirrel, *see* Grey squirrel
Starling, 69

Stock dove, 26, 32-33, 34, 49, 68
Swallow, 54, 58, 68
Sweet chestnut, 5, 16, 49. *See also* Chestnut
Swift, 54, 58-59, 68

Tawny owl, 9, 20, 32, **34**, 35-38, **37**, 49, 65, 68
Teal, 20, 69
Thrush, 11, 12, 51, 57. *See also individual species*
Tits, 27. *See also individual species*
Touraco, 1
Treecreeper, 9, 45-47, 69
Tree pipit, 55, 69
Tree sparrow, *see* Sparrow
Tufted duck, 20, 69
Turtle dove, 15, 33, 69

Vole, 29

Warbler, 52, 53, 55. *See also individual species*
Waxwing, 55, 57, 69
Wheatear, 69
Whimbrel, 21, 69
Willow warbler, 53, 69
Woodcock, 21, 69
Woodpecker, 26, 39-41, 45. *See also individual species*
Wood pigeon, 26, 30-34, **31**, 68
Wood warbler, 15, 55, 69
Wren, 10, 68
Wryneck, 62, 69

Yellowhammer, 58, 70
Yellow wagtail, 54, 69